Dislocated

by

Dylan Webster

ISBN: 978-0-578-39079-6

Published by Quillkeepers Press, LLC
PO Box 10236
Casa Grande, AZ 85130

This book is dedicated to my wife,
Esther, my closest friend, and the
one without whom this work
would never have found its way
into your hands.
Esther, thank you—for this and
for breathing life into it all.

Forward

A fervent student of wisdom at heart, with a poetic outlook that makes you ponder upon everyday life in a fresh light. His rhythm seems to shake the page, making them all the easier to turn. Whether contemplating sorrowful memories or reliving the joys of days past, this volume makes a perfect companion. Using his faith as a foundation for his outlook on the world, his love for his fellow man is evident in every piece. His writhing words create imagery that leaves behind a lasting impact on readers. Gripping their attention with a subtle embrace that gently refuses to let go. His poetry is deeply endowed with an intense passion for literature emblazoned in each stanza.

His love for writing is rivaled only by that of his marvelous family. A beautifully talented artist for a wife, alongside a caring vibrant son full of wonder and life, help to inspire such a unique style and elusive vocabulary.

As a friend, as well as a fan, I count myself blessed to have such a kindhearted selfless person who is always ready to uplift a complete stranger with genuine words of kindness in my life.

Though growing up was at times tumultuous, he sought solace in the same books he would later pen himself. Finding father figures within the writers who seemed to tell the same stories he suffered but was not ready to share. Having found his voice, he is finally prepared to spread his gift around the globe. I hope this collection finds you when needed most and brings you the same sense of relief that Dylan gives to all he comes across. This book has been a lifetime of progress, but only the beginning of such an inspiring poet for generations of dreamers to come.

—Christopher Lopez

I

II

III

IV

V

I

Pose

Peace be upon a world
that has already passed.
A copy of a falsification
is now more real than ever.
Souls spilling into unreality
come out smiling
on the other end.
Deadened lifeless eyes
glimmer in the reflection
of a million soaking eyes.
Youthful eyes now older
than the bodies that house them.
Eyes that watch the earth
as it sprints toward them
like flocks descending,
beautiful sensational birds,
dotting the earth with little graves.

Smelling Salts

If war has never been won,
we have never freed anything, anyone.
War is not where
corpses have fed the ancient trees,
where our blood has poisoned life
or where our vivified machinations
have manifested and rent God's work.
Shattering our sickened mother,
leaving all life in tatters.

Our war is in correspondence.
The mirroring of progress
along with the regression,
degradation of our will,
and the pacification of resolve.
Suffer the children—

Screams pierce the solace, we are absent.
Streams of consciousness
let out into oceans.
Foaming, fomenting the anger,
rage of imprisoned souls.
Our collectivity is absence,
writhing plagued masses
amassing vigor, strength,
stronger than reinforced steel walls
sunken beneath the nation's sullied White House.

Perfect Vision

All the dystopian futures
joined hands in cacophonous orgy,
while you and I watched them become one
hideous malformed abject misery personified.
Their temple of flesh has iced over in black decay,
and my throat vomits blood from screaming at an
ambivalent sky.

Awoken

Smother the ghosts
of insecurity
with supernatural
determination—
expelling my heart
in ink
as I exorcize—
demonic, this dark
entity
cowers before me.

Simulacrum

Your speech has become
a vague shadow
stricken with pallor.
A lost memory
of the intent
that bore it.

Heartbeat Clocks

Is time bound to hands
gliding on clocks
or bits rearranging to shapes of numbers?
Is time bound to rivets that cut
into my face and whither my hands?
Is time bound to when I punch in
and when I punch out—
to how much was produced
and how long it took?
Is time bound to how much I can do
before I'm displayed in cedar
within a cathedral
to be baptized again by the tears
of my progeny?

Could not time be now
and then,
when,
and everywhere—

How much time was lost reading this?
Or
How much time was gained
by
Hearing me?

You are time,
we are time,
this is time—

spend us wisely.

Blasphemy

Rugged feet depress fresh grass as they ascend.
This man rising above the throng of people
to deliver words that will be immortalized.

His back collects beads of oily sweat
as his body moves against the ancient sun
that his followers say he made himself.

The edges of his ragged robes tear further,
and calloused feet wear down his old sandals.

His hair is matted to his forehead
as he reaches the height of the hill.

A whore sits near him,
adoringly listening to his words
as the men questioningly watch her,
wary of her malicious motives.

This blasphemer speaks humanity
to weary people thirsty for justice
and dreaming of equality.

Uneducated working-class lowlifes
make up this man's movement.

Women finance his every need.
Men obediently attend to his words.

The whore at his right hand closes her eyes,
and I often wonder if she knew
that she'd be cast as the reformed
sex addict.

Peter questions the man,
and I often wonder if he questioned
what would become of this movement.

Hegemony

Speak clearly.
Think soberly.
Act properly
in accordance
with
my speech, thought
and action
hegemonic.
I am your master,
your lover, logic
and
life.

Projections

Closure is
the lie
they tell us to
give us hope that'll
never be returned.
Maybe, striving against wind
ever fervent,
we'll find something to revive these
hearts,
these hollow husks.
Life's
heart-stopping moments
stopped for far
too long.

Vantage Point

The lines between abstractions
have fallen out of view—
I've mixed up all the concepts.
The tidy boxes have disintegrated
along with my sensibilities.

I no longer always know
how to discern the waves
from the horizon.

It seems to me we're uncertain
as when to feel any emotion.
The tide is coming in—

I know what's left of my boxes
will be reclaimed by the waves.
What I don't know
is what I should be feeling

as the retreating tide
erodes the granules of earth
from beneath my toes.

The Work of Our Hands

Ether in its oceanic
vastness
rent asunder by
machinations—
children of men
procreating
with metal and veins of
Wire,
coursing with the new
blood—
dishonor breeds with pride
begetting our Reapers—
judgement
very seldom is
just.
We are Titans
Indeed,
But lo, we breathe life into
Olympians.

Solitary Thoughts

I've conjured mental monsters
grotesque in their shapelessness
phantasmagoria in a realm unbound—
ghosts whispering aphorisms of decay
eroding the foundations of my image—
behind the eyes are phantoms
in a personal Erebus
much worse than
demons in hell.

Canticle

I saw a figure slogging through darkness
as if through overgrowth knee high
sloughing something off shrugging shoulders.

a shadow among thicker shadows
like darkness contrasted by
darker blackness.

And at the end of this vision,
the shadow figure dissipated
with hands reaching skyward;

a lighter darkness, canopy overhead,
and in the quiet of the blackness becoming
a nascent grey ascending higher,

I heard the slightest whisper of singing.

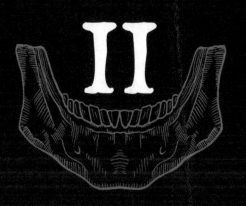

Etchings

Scripture
sounds sacred
when spoken out loud—
but the word only means
writings,
scribblings—
if that is true
then is what we scrawl
not scripture, too?
Is it not
our souls' scriptures
being breathed as we speak,
being birthed as we feel,
sinews wrapping round bone
and flesh, encasing these
spiritual spirals of thought?
Sacred synapses indeed.

The Prophecies

To whom can we turn
to save us from evil?
Deliver us in this,
our dark and gloomy
hour!

We cry for help,
and cry ourselves to sleep—
we cry out to —

the frighteningly vast sky
ever gray, indifferent,
bereft of love,
long since derelict,
the home only
of the object of hate.

We look around
to fellow humankind!
Yes, so good and
compassionate and willing—

but where are you,
my siblings?

Our last remaining hope
are the ones with blades in hand,
they lurk in the shadows
and slay us in prayer.

Our last remaining hope
is none other than
the Enemy.

For we have killed
all divine recourse,
and now rush to blot out
all memory thereof.

We were warned,
we've been warned,
prophets of the earth
have sung their warning songs,
calling our attention to
the Devil,
devils,
evil demons
of destruction.

The sacrilegious sapiens.
Nothing is holy
and nothing is pure now,
nothing is good,
and are the prophecies truly clear,
that someone will save us,
rescuing us from our own
Hands?

Falsified

Deepen your senses
with deadened nerves
as touch means less
each day that passes —

each moment filled
with paradox
where once euphoria,
in cascading explosions,
racked your spine, tightened your skin,
Goosebump trails of history —

now you fight harder
bite deeper
into numbed flesh.

Monstrosity

The earth is more than full—
subdued through murderous lust
as her children trample her,
enraptured by illusions
of luxury and ease;

they poison their mother
while exploiting her fruits—
warn the children from youth
and teach them rhymes,
teach them myths — how fantastically unreal!

Yet here we are,
with matricide, conspiracy,
hatred & blood-soaked hands,
indeed, monsters walk the earth,

and now, like brothers in the field
or brothers building empires,
we turn to spill familial blood.

Matches in the Garden

I often find myself wondering
what life is like after life—
once the deja vu dissipates,
like silent slithering overcast—

once the final slumber ends in the opening
of our eyes.
Once the lethargy of lingering nightmares
finally slips into the daylight.

Perhaps, this *is* eternity
perhaps Purgatory's overpopulated
and we are dumped here again.

The purifying fires are just on the hills,
and the North Country,
and the vast swathes of quickly ending life
rather than on our bodies,
although these, too, are burning.
this, our bootleg Paradise —

we had the blank canvas before us,
& the creativity and will of gods;
but deeming Paradise too idealistic
and Purgatory so last millennium

we created Hell.

Splendor

Vapid undergrowth
in the garden
decays & drains
the life surging throughout.

Slowly,
stealthy in its murder,
the undergrowth
excels, reclaiming
fertile ground,

as the vivid
fragrant flora
lurches in travail—
a penultimate glance
at the sun in its distance

before looking upon
vile parasitic ephemera,
the vivacious jubilant murderer
that sprawls across their bed,
asphyxiating beauty in the garden.

And This Is What I Saw

Consumption—
Inhale,

eyes wide—
take it in,
toxic fumes.

Coursing through
veins,
rattle in the cerebral
arena—
a vacuum.

Sense of direction
disoriented
& the sight of others
inebriated,
senseless.

When I Was Not Who I Will Be

Worlds were found
where worlds would be found,
where they are currently being found
where they always will be found—

we will be found where we were,
where we are and where
we will be;

Murphy's law is no law at all,
never was,
it never will be—

it will be a description
(anachronistic,
but a description, nonetheless)

of what was
before itself,

and after us.

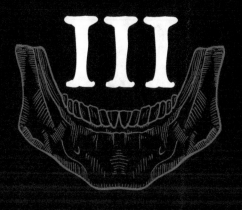

A Note on Anxiety

What is this delicious death drive
beating like relentless rain,
like dark melodies of nightclubs
filled with wandering aimless souls,
where once my heart calmed my breath?

Inverse

Straining my thoughts
just to form coherent strains,
churning, aching, clouds—
indecisive where to vomit their rain.
I'm reduced to a thinking mess,
tomes of thought compile within
while I remain
tongue tied.

The knot in my mouth
ever uncooperative,
I fix my gaze upon you all,
praying you can read the words
as they scroll down my eyes
welling with the weight,
I lurch toward your understanding,
a stumbling mute.

Sandstorm

Stressing the words
into granules of sand
I have lost my intent—
passing through my teeth
and bloodying my gums—

could I reshape them into castles,
you would see the grandeur,
but with the tide of passing time
you would behold the decay.

Perhaps I'll remain
and become the recluse
in a kingdom of dunes.

Happy

Perish the words of devils

    they said

never having seen their own Satan—

    exult in your freedom

while I remain derelict & haunted;

    return to me when you need an exorcist

and I'll watch the flames

    lick up your arrogance

vigorous like a lover

    In the dark.

Damnation

How often
has solace become sacred?

Is this healthy healing
or the halitosis of hell?

Self-care so slowly becomes
self-harm when left

alone.

Beholder

If beauty is in the eye of the beholder

where?

The cornea,
or perhaps the pupil,
nestled in the darkness
hardly perceptible?

Where?

Imperceptibly hidden
in the obscure
Whiteness,
too obvious to see.

Where?

Far too subjective
to be an object,
an abstract concept
To be cherished in the mind.

Where?

Perhaps perception
is flawed,
and it is *nowhere* hidden,
it is visibly within.

Beauty's not contained in lolling orbs.

Pregnant Pens

We hold seances,
soliloquies of the supernatural
Conjuring, and drawing out spirits
from deep within the shrouded
realm of spurious sentences—
disjointed bones of thoughts sealed—
these we release spontaneously
until through our pens we spill
dancing skeletons;
clacking in their wisdom, sempiternal.

Association

Take my hand
let's wander these
labyrinthine passages—
fragmented thought
distorted perceptions.

I cannot tell what darkness
wrought these lines within,
but with you
we could search until
the maze runs out
and find the sinuous sea;

swallow every wave
yet the thirst is never
quenched.

Valley of Shades

Undressing words
of all their meaning
would that not reduce them
to naked intent?

For some
however
the removal of masks
leaves only
ghosts.

Synapse

I write words
like dance;

I love like
torrential rain;

conversing like
English new wave;

I act like
whatever wave

of emotion

erupts through
dry intellect.

Illusory

Vices masquerading
as gods;
intoxicating
with inversely
divine
lies.

Survey

My apologies for the gloom
but, why are we joyful?

What glory is gotten
in this wasteland will
we've written?

Consider the corpses
quickly buried beneath
our blossoming blindness—

or perhaps it's nearly over?
How the Red Herring harks!
Hallowed be the sanitized halls.

What sates the soulless?
Death. Dislocated dear ones,
death. Delivered dry, dilapidated.

Why are we joyful?

Let there be hope,
but, don't trample truth
beneath tenacious truisms.

Breathing Time

The unnerving peace
that arrives at the end—
nothing is solved,
nothing is saved—
but dread has tired
and without any strength
to torment
gives birth—
paradoxical peace,
tremulous tranquility.

Beneath the Torrents

The movement of thought billows,
incense filling the sanctuary;
no stream
and little consciousness;
gradual expansion,
metamorphosing images;
scenes acted out quickly
yet, without the aid of Time—
there is only what *is;*
I cannot craft my idols
With smoke—
I inhale the vaporous incense
filling my lungs with thought ,
impressions of intuition,
like the smudged letters of a book
held fast by enthralled readers;
I am entranced by these wafting
visions, these oracles of what
whispers to us amorously
when we cease striving.

What I Meant

I scratched emotions
into eternity for you.
Yet the effect—

intentions, curious little creatures.
And I say creatures
since they so often
inhale imaginative personas

of their own and proceed
to dance on stage
in ways I did not direct.
Perceptions
also appear
to interpret and play
with intentions.

They assumed the role
of director in the play
they have written.

I sit among the audience
beside you and watch
reality in all its unintended
drama.

Architecture of Intentions

Words themselves
paint no pictures
but perceptions.
A house is built
and someone's psyche
fills and paints it
like God breathing life,
vibrant and salient.
Instead, we raise pillars
to prop up illustrious ceilings
yet the tapestry is woven by others.

Mediators

Pens across the world
etch hope into existence,
and souls across world
transform hope to action.

Languishing spirits
haunt streets at night
and revive deadened hearts.

As the gulf between us
matures into an abyss,
I pray these pens
become more prolific
and these specters
bridge the gap.

Disparate

Is it any surprise
that spirit is feminine?
I seek the truth
while fighting the
womb of warmth.

Attestation

Flesh stripped from words
leaves bones and sinews
laid bare, laden with truth—
how couldn't we know
that your blood lent
life to lyrics?

Discord

These competing voices clamor
within my house, my mind,
ever screaming louder
And to what end?

These voices crescendo
in a maelstrom unbearable
but more unbearable still
is their silence.

Dust gathers like snow
upon now antique furnishings
as what once was lively
now sleeps,

ignorant of the ephemera
I sought to kill the clamor,
but I hadn't known that
sometimes
the negative space
makes the masterpiece,
and silence and serenity aren't
always synonyms skipping hand in hand.

The clamor, though clamorous, became
comforting white noise to lull a troubled heart.

Derelict souls now have so many
kindred spirits
assailed by a silence thick

as the insulation between the bones
of our houses.
Now I never wonder
what reasons
impel the actions—

the voices clamor.
Empathetic
voices rising, erratic
from years of silence,
discordant
melting into one—
revivified.

Breviloquent

They say to brandish yourself like lightning.
To splash onto the frontpage.
Speak your truth and let your song be sung.

But loquacious though you may be,
you remain unseen and unheard.

Inconsequential as your throat grows red
with didactic reflux.
Within despair however,
you may find your terse truth

and recognize the power
of blunt pithiness.

Maybe you won't flash
like the electric explosions,
but, thunder rattles
the earth—

Absurd

Careening from task to task,
breathless.
Trying to hold dying leaves.
Seeking to see their colors
before they litter the ground.
mummified.

Ascend the tree,
ever so ancient,
and cradle its children

or flit away with them,
wafting between heaven and
Earth,
your home,
your grave.

Something in the descent—
the in-between
is where beauty
deifies.

Betwixt heav'n and earth—
there is the Divine
in the cadence of fallen
leaves.

Dissident

An awkward gait limping,
lumbering along as you think

like a tongue scraping stucco,

Legs unwilling to yield to volition,
volatile with every step forward—

My brain is a cripple,

and it's to *It* that I speak
scream, rather, while it dances

knife edge ready to penetrate.

Intuition

When fear
grows talons
and slithers them
around your throat—
you know it's right.

De Profundis

Writing my soul
closer to divinity,
ascending
by first falling
into the depths—
finding the words
among images,
among shadows
serenading my spirit
into a trance—
transcendence via
introversion.

Listening to the Wind

Words of wisdom
whispered from
the edge of society,
seers, sages, and singers
weaving the cosmos
into a tapestry diverse
as the very universe
whose hymn they
compose—
an unwilling audience,
uninterested, apathetic;
apropos of the skeletons
to whom Ezekiel preached...
Let us pray the sinews
reconnect our lost bones,
and those words carry the Breath
of Life,
the Pneuma unseen,
yet ever felt within us
all.

A Stirring Thought

Brutalizing hearts
with forceful truth,
the strongest kiss
with biting teeth,
the bone crushing
embrace of passion—
set these minds ablaze
and let's burn

                  burn

          burn—
incinerate the icy doubt
that frosts these souls,
that numbs these lives
till blades on skin
cause no pain.

Odes and Ballads Are So Last Century

I dehydrate my pen
attempting to grasp
your visage—
languishing in its
bloodletting
as it gives its soul
over to your beauty.

Inaction

Days meld together
cyclical, my aspirations
ever flirting with time
imagining inevitable acclaim—

my thoughts iridescent
in their creative longings,
luminous art birthed in my mind—

spirits and souls touched deeply
by my words in these mental interactions—

all the while I remain seated, dreaming,

distracted

Debilitating

Glisten in the

light

of your
words, your

thoughts

not all that you do
is wrong, selfish
weak or imitation—

destroy

the voice within
whispering malformed
hatred, the lies of
your mind to your heart—

destroy.

Interior Life

The volatility within us—
the opportunity,
and capacity—
the spectrum of emotion
from rage
to empathy—
an ecosystem of
impressions & sensations.
What beautifully fragile,
Spasmodic worlds
We create.

Anxiety

The implosion of self-worth
the crumbling of walls
we threw up for protection.—

The universe spinning backwards,
uncreating all that is seen and touched,
clocks rewinding to zero.

Oceans retrieving the waves given
draining themselves of life,
evaporating through unshielded skies—

leaves withering and shrinking,
sinking back into their mother trees,
until even they are but seeds.

Apostate

How tiresome it becomes
to edit and hand you
all my redacted thoughts—
my censored soul,
so as to preserve
this effigy of ego
you've carelessly constructed.

Your presence rarely granted,
and only upon meeting
at the altar in your temple—
the verbose coward,
thin-skinned judge
on his tremulous throne!

The only incense I'll burn
are the miles of worn pages,
your tomes of arrogance—
and fill the alms-baskets
with ash.

Spatial Awareness

Like the displacement
of imploding stars,
cosmic wells of light—
endless and unknown
& undiscovered—

so the thoughts
of suffering souls
with brilliant eyes
burning their final
Supernovas.

Gaze into their
constellations,
and behold their
divine humanity—
lest they become another

pinhole in the universe.

Brilliance

Stars displaced, we descend
in realms without compasses,
in the darkness informed by absence;

were we not the locus,
the pull, irresistible, blind,
and powerful? Were we not creation's
darling children? No, indeed, more;

we were the precursors to gods,
we dwell in heavens, only the fringes of which
lower life is deluded to think it knows,

bewitched; but we, no, we were true,
real, and visible regardless of desire;

yet we fall, eaten up;
buckling beneath and into ourselves.

Soul

Bleed the darkest you can
for it makes the truest color—
dip the brush,
soiled thistles
and scrape it along canvas—
oxblood images conjured
and breathe their scarlet life.
For the life is in the blood.
To excoriate is to remove hearts.
Now let us build maroon cathedrals
guarded by our bloody canvas hounds.

Imagination

You see the images parading
before our eyes,
we both stand
here.

But once we recount the visage,
we tell divergent
tales of sight &
reality.

Respiration

Ever aging in moments that seem already past,
running childlike to grab hold of clouds,
I find the time in the hourglass kissing me
like Judas,

But allowing the betrayals to slip
like sand down to the other end
I find solace in the selfsame phantom
like death,

like Tom when I arrived at the hospital,
missing a soul by mere minutes,
gazing above as if to see his soul
like angels,

rising above to a bliss unseen & unfelt,
and in that comfort within finality, I found
the horrifying unchangeability,
like faith.

The Fear of Shadows

Your words arrive
derelict

Stripped of meaning
hollow

Shielded by vague
smoke—

Yet once cleared
(*revelation*)

You're left standing
skeletal.

Darkroom

Shall we strike a match
in the darkness of will?
The flickering light
haphazardly reverberating shadows
won't lighten the weight of life
that disassembles vertebrae.
The horror coming into vision
does not diminish the monsters.

stand, breathe shallow,
and peer into freedom —
if your wits still become you,
I beg you
take my hand,
teach me.

Bearing Gifts

Bury my words deep
like charred ashen runes
beneath the saltiness of deadened leaves—

brush the muddied red and brown aside
and blacken the tips of your fingers
with my fallen incantations—

use the earthy clay to drape these runes
and turn them to holy rubrics
for my coffin worn words
are now yours.

The Baggage

I felt bonds like chains
fastened upon my wrists;

metal scraping scraps
of me
away, flaking into nothing.

I felt the weight
of religions and eons,

like the weight of heaven's
expectations,
gazing upon me.

I felt the duty of honor,
of holy obligation,

because it wasn't your blood
bluing my veins,
but it was your presence

blackening my heart;

a false altar upon which

my blood still glistens.

Ancestral

Do the salt thickened winds
of Scotland fill my lungs
as they did for my grandfather's
father? Is this my heirloom
bequeathed through blood?

From him and his fathers
I've received a love for the sea.
Your face I have never seen,
but I see your spirit glimmer
in the eyes of my mother's father.

Does spirit surge in blood,
that four generations
after your Scottish birth
a Mexican-American three-year-old
grins with brilliant joy
on a boat in California?

How can a father's son
have a character like an ancestor
he has never seen?
as when I met my great-grandmother
on my father's side,
delighting her with the mannerisms

of a man a lifetime unknown,
as he too resembles men
only she remembers, long passed.

I hardly know him
and yet his gifts course
through my veins.

Vision

Why are some moments so pregnant?
Minds expanding.
phasing through brains
and skulls;

dropping screens with vivid scenes
down low, draped over eyes
that see the phenomenal.

A sip of coffee at a workstation
mindlessly completing tasks
while tallying the minutes

until my momentary recreation—
but now that sip of warm bitterness
wearing the clothing of light caramel
becomes just one sip amid
a philosophical discussion about things,

with capitals
while tallying minutes becomes
watching Time as a stream ebb and flow,
and swell and overcome and recede—
thinking about how these spectacles
of perception we wear color this world
we all see, touch and smell and—

that other thing. The thing that baffles
the thing that dwells in the Abyss,
and sometimes looks seductive,
like the Absurd personified,
or perhaps like Personification herself

Previously Published Credits

"Vantage Point" has been published in Quillkeepers Press *Turning Dark into Light...and Other Magic Tricks of the Mind*
Mental Health Anthology May 2021

"Absurd" has been published in *The Cannons Mouth Quarterly Issue 81 September 2021*

"Breviloquent" has been published in *The Dillydoun Review Issue 2.1 March 2021*

"Canticle" has been published in the Dillydoun Review Issue 11 December 2021.

Dislocated

Acknowledgements

There are so many people to thank, but I have to start with my family. The support of my wife, Esther, to whom this was dedicated. You have had the single largest impact on my writing. It was dead and lay languishing for years, and upon just your words alone, it leapt to life again. You put up with it all, not only pretty, but also the ugly. The words just for me to grow, that only you know. I love you.

Also, my brother for reading so many pieces against his will since he was ten. I would like to thank my grandparents for their support ever since I told them I like to write, from buying me books to reading my work. You are a brilliant example of lives well lived, full of joy and wonder and laughter. Also, to my son, you have no idea how much you inspire me, thank you, for bursting with life at all times.

I'd like to thank Gail Comer for reading my poetry and discussing lyricism with me. As well as Marc Taylor, one of my closest friends, for critiquing and reading over my poetry, even when they were sent at midnight. You gave insights that affected this collection more than you know. Thank you.

Chris Lopez for embarking on reading journeys and trying to figure out just how old our souls really are;

you breathe new life into those you love and have become an example of realizing one's potential. I'd also like to thank my other friends, Kris McCall, Chris Nagamine, who read and critiqued most of these poems, Kweku Shaw Jones, Brandon Kovacs, Alexandria Yeruslan, Gabrielle Beam, and too many others to list.

Thank you to Samieh, for taking my picture.

Lastly, to all the people at Quillkeepers' Press who alchemically turned dreams into matter. Especially the incredibly talented Stephanie Lamb, who saw something in the very first submission I sent and realized a dream I'd had for such a long time. But then continued to believe in me and fan the creative flame that was so precarious before. I truly cannot thank you enough for all that you have done, and I look forward to partnering with you again in the future. You are unique and strong and kind, a combination rarely seen upon this earth.

Dylan becomes lost in tales of the mind, and the worlds that can be contained within it. He seeks to photograph these scenes in poetry. He enjoys writing fiction as well and is working on his first novel. He reads many things but often finds himself in the works of past centuries, where lamps were powered by gas, and the main means of travel was in a carriage, the clacking of horse hooves beating the dusty road.

Dear Reader,

Thank you for delving into the psyche of a stranger. I hope that within these pieces, you find glimpses of yourself and those you know. For fifteen years I dreamed of the day that a collection of these mental images would be read by you, and now I set to work to bring you more.

Dislocated

What Others are Saying About *Dislocated*

"Dylan Webster's first poetry collection *Dislocated* reads like a raw, impassioned cry to the often-ambivalent masses to wake up 'and in the quiet of blackness becoming/ a nascent grey ascending higher, [hear] the slightest whisper of singing.' *Dislocated* skillfully invites us to explore the modern scripture of our collective soul and to question abstraction. Webster expunges his own demons with introspection and grace while artfully giving the reader plenty of room to run into the forest of his words and unearth their own shadow selves. An accomplished, fervent first effort by Dylan Webster."

—Amy Burns
Author of *Leaving is My Colour*
Editor-in-Chief of *The Dillydoun Review)*

"Dylan Webster's poems in *Dislocated* are clear-sighted and courageous lyric meditations. In an earnest, sober tone, the poet explores the condition of the world and his own limitations, as he carries out his call of being a writer. *Dislocated* is firmly located in the complexities of the here and now with rising expectation, faith, and hope—'the slightest whisper of singing.'"

—Aaron Caycedo-Kimura
Author of *Ubasute* and forthcoming *Common Grace*

"Dylan Webster writes like a man juggling kerosene lanterns: spectacular, dangerous, putting on a show. The poems in *Dislocated* are fiery, but also awe-inspiring. They explore extremes of war and peace, good and evil, sacred and profane, without losing their sense of fun. The shorter poems, especially, are intense little explosions. This collection serves as a strong debut by a poet to watch."

—Ace Boggess
Author of *Escape Envy* and *The Prisoners*

"Dylan has written a searching, ambitious first work in conversation with the greats of the Western canon. His love of form and craft is reflected in every poem."

—Clementine Von Radics
Author of *Home* and *Dream Girl*
For Teenage Girls with Wild Ambitions and Trembling Hearts and *In a Dream You Saw a Way to Survive*
A Whore's Manifesto: An Anthology of Writing and Artwork by Sex Workers and *Mouthfuls of Forevers*